Genesis: In the beginning of October

Jonny Cosmo

BookLeaf
Publishing

India | USA | UK

Genesis: In the beginning of October © 2021
Jonny Cosmo

All rights reserved.

Presentation by *BookLeaf Publishing*

Web: www.bookleafpub.com

E-mail: info@bookleafpub.com

ISBN : 9789357448246

First edition 2021

DEDICATION

Dedicate to those brave enough to read past the first page.

I love you.

ACKNOWLEDGEMENT

Thanks to Emma for telling me about this.

You absolute Queen.

And to Ali for the AI Ainspiration.

PREFACE

A random short assortment of thoughts day to
day.

01/10/21 - 21/10/21

to be - 01/10/21

Try not to live a life of ease
Are you with yours anymore pleased
You can start anytime and turn a new leaf
Stories are better off the skin of your teeth

A lesson learned is one that we keep
Praise those who got here by their feet
Respect the withered old lone dead tree
For its roots hold a history it may never set free

Go wherever people wont be
Adventure far but be back for tea
Open your mind if you want to see
The greatest answers are questions of mystery

PU~NK - 02/10/21

Thinking about the evolution of punk...

Born out of the era of counterculture hippies and funk,
but some saw it was less flower and rainbows
and more chains and skulls.

Cool became cool then it became pop,
just to state that was the death of avant garde
(pop-art killed avant garde)...
Pop punk was born, Boys leading men, Girls
leading women it was a devolving trend,
if you tried you're a poser as if anything isn't
pretend

Post-modernism had to lead to post-punk,
I'm angry at the state and I still love ma mum.
I can see where we're going and I can see from
where we've come
but I'll shout loud to change that path until the
working class has won.

Call yourself punk but you feed the machine
I don't give a fuck if you need it to eat
The idea is ruckus rather than sleep

Other wise they fuck us like the welsh n' the
sheep

At my age - 03/10/21

At my age
What the fuck does that even mean at my age
At my age I should have...

At my age there's People with houses and
without...

At my age there's People pissed everyday and
some never had a drop

At my age there's People doing pornography
And the ones that pay for 'em to do it

At my age there's church goers and tea drinkers
but also stoners and pill takers

At my age there's those who meditate and those
who are told they need to medicate

At my age there's those with 4 kids and those
who are still virgins

At my age there's those on their 4th car and
those without a license

5

At my age there's those in the know and those
who don't

At my age you've got smokers and tokers those
who work in casinos those who play poker

At my age
What the fuck do you mean at my age

Playing with your thoughts - 04/10/21

Realised that I cannot sleep
Without at least a wank or a drink

Whereas its lucky for some
Those who fuck
Or cuddled up to the ones that they love

Whereas some
Want but cannot be touched
Out of fear that in giving yourself
You're giving too much

Awake
In hope that with a bit of luck
That I'll once again be able to give a fuck

Portrait Comp - 05/10/21

Faces of strangers
Paints the walls
Of the cafe

Kayleigh plays
Not chains
But dreams

Sunshine sung
Nods
Stomping feet

Infinite Strings - 06/10/21

Infinite Strings
That push and pull
Guide me in time
I am the leaf on the wind
I am the feather upon the surface or the river
I am the water droplet
Falling down the window pain
Guided by my predecessors
Making lines all the same
I am wind
I am time
I am water
I am life
I am
Until I'm not

Law is an old bastard - 07/10/21

Ain't the law a right old bastard
To say you couldn't slap a bag head that just
needed slapping
Cuz we split our taxes so we can feed our
countries families
But some go to feeding some scums crack habits

Of course I'm on about those who can afford it
You know the ones, blue tie, ivory tower, Tories.
Cuz for a rainy country this trickle down
economics ain't pouring.
And frankly I can't even find their propagated
statements boring.

I'm fuckin' angry
Like a smackhead gettin' aggy
We need food, shelter, water. Not enough for
another baggy.
The thing is we all know why some have these
habits
It's because the job center likes to keep 'em
captive.

30p for each pound you make
Cuz they took it back then blamed it on those
who immigrate
I'm sick of lies this isn't fate
Raise a fist proudly if you've love to give and
peace to make

Get saddened
By lack of mental health support
Yet voters stay thankful
Because their TV builds with them rapport
Telling them their class is a handful

Not for the likes of us
As basic rights are sold as luxuries
It's like Orwell's 1984 meets Brave New World
by Huxley

Academia staples motivation for lack of equity
in western nations
International meritocracy but corporations own
public property
Philosophies come from the likes of Socrates to
justify state sovereignty and take away your own
autonomy

If you give the donkey the carrot off the stick
It won't run

Because all the people are to the elite
Are mules whose minds are to be won
Even our psyches are a thing to be conquered
Is a whole life spent fighting
{Really} A whole life squandered?

Last time I tried - 08/10/21

Last time I tried to be determined
This time I'm determined not to try
Well isn't that the ironic facticity of life

I made eye contact with a fly
1000 eyes but less than 1000 days to die
Do you think it tries

If you can try
You can win or lose
If you do
There is only what you did or do

What is sexuality - 09/10/21

What is sexuality?
Different to preference for ethnicity
Without fetishising any aspect of humanity
What is sexuality?

Think about it differently
That doesn't mean being non-binary
Only a recognition of fluidity
To distinguish sex and do so lovingly

Sex, gender and love
What is sexuality?

To defy all of the imaginary
Seeing a soul rather than a body

But still preference doesn't mean sexuality
What is sexuality?

Labels only to tick a category
Over here in this demography

Stay put in this community
Division of love isn't unity

Where is the human beauty
Not a gendered aesthetic
big dick or booty
Jawlines and boobies
long hugs and spooning
a smile that is moving

What is sexuality?

Should I label those I hug?

Should I label those I fuck?

Should I label those I love?

What is sexuality?

Nothing that can be spoken of by human
rationality
Throw away the box allow the paradox of the
antinomy
Two souls touch and they cause an immortal
symphony

I ask again, what is sexuality?
And you say

it shouldn't matter to me

15

Principe - 10/10/21

Men who live by their principles, die by their principles.
Men who's principles bend, live to lie again.

Fighting the ego - 11/10/21

Been fighting my mental health
Stuck against an ego thing
So I hope I don't start mumbling
Speaking words but start stuttering
I am not muttering
Nothingness
Stage freight then I'm crumbling
Boredom strikes thumbs thumbling
If I fall then I'm tumbling
Tinder shite so I'm bumbeling
Hungry for more stomach rumbling
That was enough now it's grumbling
Sleeping it off I am slumbering
Laboring work is so lumbering
My brain is always malfunctioning
The results of effort so humbling
But I am still struggling
I'm on a path but I'm tunneling
Motivation lacks so I'm summoning
Holistic approaches all encompassing
Everything that I am Juggling
To be my better self I find troubling

I'd be lying if I said I wasn't hustling
My fuel is appreciation and I'm guzzling
Life is a test but I find the test puzzling
I may be moving forward that doesn't mean I'm
not struggling

Fall - 12/10/21

Have you ever seen a big gust of wind strip the
trees of their now orange leaves
Time of change, autumn and spring
Preparing for long nights or long days
I don't know why we don't live around these
Ways as the seasons change
Following the trees

End of the world 👎 😎🙌 - 13/10/21

What's the deal with all these little yellow faces
Emojis Bitmojis
But hand gestures have to match races
Representation served symbolically as a
hieroglyph
A concession to oppression no real change in the
pantheon

How dull must our speech be
I need to emote it with a smiley face or
aubergine
When speaking freely
But that's not good for social marketting

Media means illusion purfusely deluded the
institution is abusive watch like super hero
movies

Marvel at stupid
Kids shot and it ain't cupid

Cute is now putrid
Are we winning or losing

Ruled by the ruling
Fooled by the foolish
Schooled only rudely
Lies are fuckin' soothing

Unfree at our choosing
Flames high but I'm grooving
World still but I'm moving
Out of sync but I'm tuning

In the deep sleep where the elite feast upon the
weak I refer to them not as sheep because people
are not meat

Dead friends
14/10/21

You know those friends
Those that'd be late to their own funeral
I keep seeing them everywhere
Late to their own funerals
Even if they aren't anywhere to be seen
Is this a problem?
That I see the faces of loves lost upon the
silhouettes of strangers
Or does it just go to show
I have loves
That I've not lost

Concrete Jungle
15/10/21

Monstrous monoliths,
Glass and steel obelisks
Blocks of flats and offices
Tram lines, old bridges
Tourists taking pictures
Canals filled with rubbish
Streets, tides, waves of people flooding
All watching not listening
On their face phone Screens glistening
Staying hidden from the surroundings theyre in

I love and I Fear Big cities
As an empath I'm really intune to energy
So I don't like being surrounded by busy
As much as I find it hard to sit still and just be
I still do silently
Maybe with lofi beats and a pot of tea
There's no silence in tall walls of the city
Gutters channeling people is why it's so gritty
Civilised pity

Objective - 16/10/21

Reality sits between truth
See we can disagree
Therefore what is true for me
Isn't what is true for you

If you're asking about objectivity
You could argue there is no truth
See there's reality and there's perception
We make both our own

We exist
And that's the end of it
Although we don't
And then in the end we don't exist

There's no practicality
In deciphering reality
Only
To let it be

Stoic Gratitude - 17/10/21

Water when thirsty feels like champagne when you've earned it

Pulled a pen from the lake - 18/10/21

Medicate with a lofi playlist for ambience
Meditate to demonstrate my own transience
Procrastinate against that which I hate
impatience
Is it too late to find my own piece of happiness

Is it too late to find my own piece of happiness

Is it too late to find my own piece of
happinessssss

Break waves my voice a thunder clap I make the
ground shake
Move with the majesty of one thousand before
me
History in the making by each breath I'm taking
Pain staking onward broken glass inhaling
Internal voices wailing pointing to Dragons that
I'm chasing because I'm something in the
making by George I am slaying things I'm
faking not to chase created by my own faith.

But I walk at my own pace, my own path, in a
shared place. Spit blood with a straight face.
Save severity for cunning snakes. Break the ice
but don't humiliate. Bite the bait but don't let
them 'em degradate. There's more opportunities
than that which is already late. What's ahead is
the sake.
What's behind is what makes. Leave legacy in
your wake or forget about any trace. Live the life
you want to make. I pulled a Pen out of a Lake.
And sealed my fate. Wont blow up less I
detonate.

Crowded - 19/10/21

Everyone getting Married and having kids,
owning homes.

Im Just here tryna do my diss
Tryna get a 6 pack
Be a better me
Publish two books at once
Keep performing poetry
Working on Projects with creatives
In and for the community
Pushing my limitations for new possibilities
Understand life
Understand mind
Understand society and economics
Make use of my time
Tryna stay healthy
Tryna sleep well
Tryna develop wellness
Tryna be my Best self
Learning a language
Learning guitar
Learning psychology
Replacing whatever soft with hard
Keep a social life
Keep a sex life

Keep an online presence
Keep from depersonalise
Gonna get my name out
Gonna go far
Gonna be known
Gonna make a mark
Forgetting tough times
Forgetting toxic People
Forgetting Bad decisions
Forgetting being born evil
Reading to write
Writing to speak
Speaking to fight
Fighting to win
Rising above
Never looking down
Using my hands
To pick those up from the ground

AI Algorithm Assisted - 20/10/21

I don't fear on the watch itself
I shall see it's no try, I want what goes in sand
I know what is eternal in deep Fuck you
You be it anyway, because mine, casually but I
hate conversation.
Have habit it is that holding truth
At uni I might be stuck
Then I just floodle flowers
More funerals
See being weak
I write poetry
Hit a sad and relearn to walk. At one in
weakness
When in times home to eat and juicey pretty
things
I am a little bit sick of having no sense
I may not be able to sleep
And when I'm not I'll wake up and walk
On the edge of the night
Now my body is sick of it.
And I think sometimes I'll have to put up with it
I can't stay in the moment.

I know how much I hate my body
I'm tired
I'm just too tired.
I'm tired.
I'm so tired.
I'm so tired.
I know it's not going to work
I don't want to get on my own
I'm tired.I'm tired.I'm tired.I'm tired.I'm tired.I'm
tired.I'm tired.I'm tired.I'm tired.I'm tired.I'm
tired.I'm tired.I'm tired.I'm tired.I'm tired.I'm
tired.I'm tired.I'm tired.I'm tired.I'm tired.I'm
tired.I'm tired.I'm tired.I'm tired.I'm tired.I'm
tired.I'm tired.I'm tired.I'm tired.I'm tired.I'm
tired.I'm tired.I'm tired.I'm tired.I'm tired.

Consluive Seasons - 21/10/21

And the Summer comes to a close
Under a new name some call fall
Time to sew the harvest fill up the store
Ubiquitous energy changes all in synchronicity
Moon in full times ten
New beginnings means old ends